A Divine Psyche Manifesto

1990/2016

& other poems

A Divine Psyche Manifesto

1990/2016

& other poems

Ron Lampi

Felton, California

A Divine Psyche Manifesto
Copyright © 2016 by Ron Lampi
www.ronlampi.com

All rights reserved. No part of this book may be reproduced, stored in a retrieval system, or transmitted, in any form or by any means, electronic, mechanical, photocopying, recording, or otherwise, without the written prior permission of the author, except in the case of brief quotations embodied in critical articles and reviews.

Design by River Sanctuary Graphic Arts

Soul Talk series No.16-104

Printed in the United States of America

ISBN 978-1-935914-71-6

Additional copies are available from:

www.riversanctuarypublishing.com

www.ronlampi.com

RIVER SANCTUARY PUBLISHING
P.O Box 1561
Felton, CA 95018
www.riversanctuarypublishing.com
Dedicated to the awakening of the New Earth

Other works by Ron Lampi

Bay of Monterey, Poems of Monterey Bay 2010
Toward The Mythos, philosophical essays 2010
Lamp Light, A selection of short poems 2nd ed. 2011

Also published by River Sanctuary Publishing:

From the Corridors (of the Labyrinth) 2011
The New Story, Two Poems 2011
The Poet Reflects 2012
On The Cruz, Poems of Santa Cruz 2012
Through the Labyrinth 2013
Poetry / Is 2013
The Vision of Psyche & other poems 2015

Contents

A Divine Psyche Manifesto	1
The Answer	7
The Vision Starts Here	9
I Celebrate the Lightworker	13
We, The Aquarians	15
Legend Makers	20
The Transformer	21
To Heal the Planet	23
Faith	25
She will cast Her net...	28
When you hear this tone	29

All of the poems in this short work are taken from the massive collection titled *Advent*, which, as of this date March 2016, has not yet been published. Those who would want a better understanding of my experience with Psyche, and what I am sharing as Psyche, should become familiar with *The Vision of Psyche & other poems*, also published by River Sanctuary Publishing.

A Divine Psyche Manifesto

With disgust & with anger I look back on these long years
    of our silence,
these years without Passion, years without Vision,
these pedestrian sidewalk molasses years numbing of anticlimactic
    Postmodern blahs,
these years of an intolerably stressed out, sclerotic, propagandized nation
lulled by the Big Lie—
    Lie of the media tube's slick Teflon Fabrication.
    Lie of the mouth-frothing, Spirit-castrating, Satan-baiting,
        God-in-a-box Fundamentalists.
    Lie of the stainless steel, silicon-injectable old paradigm ideal,
        the endless feel good progress of Technos.
    Lie of the you-can-have-it-all yuppie wet dreams in consumer heaven,
        mountains of big daddy dollars waiting at the end of a self-
        deluding, lullaby-to-sleep rainbow.
    Lie of the Power Establishment's smoke & mirrors, its cover-ups
        & catered corridors of spin handlers & secret consultants
        & image-marketing specialists fashioning the golem
        of deceit & deception & disinformation.

Years of lies! cover-ups! deceit & deception & disinformation!
media minions packaging sound-bite placebos
—the medium is the message, goes the electro-sage maxim,
    unreality dished up on instant TV dinner platters—
& our forgotten spiritual energies are dammed up
like real atomic power in a somatic containment underground
by conditioned insecurity of Ego, our slick narcissistic little dictator,
its gray matter reduced to a fetid mass of resumes—

    IT IS TIME
    IT IS TIME TO OPEN OUR EYES
    IT IS TIME TO LET A NEW POWER COME THROUGH

I open my eyes & the American billboard I see—
I see hordes of buzz word simpletons & interfacing clueless geeks,
    fashion robots & lobotomized rats banging heads into the walls
    of their maze, reptile survivalists & sad rooms filled
    with obedient zombies of TV.
I see multitudes vomiting the microwave gibberish of hype.
I see new generations cowering & prostrate before the monstrosity
    of Hydra, triple-headed of Career, Money & Security.
I see new university-bred barbarians loyal to no one but their own
    vengeful, life-is-tough self-interest.
I see sprawling suburb armies, marching mindless to the mantra
    of success, tagging along their flash card two-year-olds.
I see long-planned Pentagon war game strategists setting ever-new
    dates for Armageddon.
I see our B-movie street violent decline, our nerve-shot gasp
    & collapse, our blood-letting hunger,
    our
        dis-
            orientation
                    the homeless tide
            no beacon
                to see by
    always awaiting the next war
                preparing now for
                      setting a date for...

    & the people perish, without a Vision.

People! Fellow Americans! Citizens of the world!
Did we not have a Dream? A Dream of our Mother planet
turning to a new dawn, turning to the Sun to celebrate
our long-awaited soul liberation, the Golden Light promise
    of the Aquarian?
Has the Dream been betrayed?
Must we suffer a Dark Age?

Too long has Divine Power within breast & skull been forgotten.
Too long our tired disappointment over some past psychedelic revolution half-baked.
Too long have we been duped by our own disillusionment, falling prey to the cynic sycophants of the Grand Media behind-the-curtain Fabricator.

 Are we cowards? Can we not keep our eyes open?
 Can we not praise new Vision in our midst?
 Let us say it: Our cynicism is rot.

There is another Song in the Air—
Hear it? I sing it—

From the long-readied tongue a new Word goes forth—
I have stood prepared upon the far, eye-casting Pacific cliffs of Vision
 & I have heard it rise, rise melodious from the sea—
Swift, potent, mercurial, revealing futurity, transforming the willing heart that receives it.
A Word like a wind of Fire, penetrating the steel casing of the brain, cement embankments of the flesh, lead walls of the heart, re-circuiting the new silicon digital eyes & ears.
A Word like a wind of Fire, liberating the bodiless imprisoned voices repressed for centuries by Church of Sin & Church of Science, voices of all your animal shadows & totems, your complexes, neuroses, hang-ups, howling within you.
A Word like a wind of Fire, melting the daily prison bars of your credit, cosmetics, cars & computers, your television & endless videos, your guns & cocaine & valium, your compulsive Wall Street connection.
A Word like a wind of Fire, addressing the anthill multitudes swarming & swarming daily the freeways, city plazas, stadiums, shopping malls & airports,
addressing you, the naked individual, in your midnight solitudes, insomniacs of your fears & insecurities, your vertigo before the abyss of your soul—
Do you turn away? We have turned away long enough.

From the poet's tongue a new Word goes forth,
like a wind of Fire bearing the tiny Seed of a new spiritual urgency—
A Seed you cannot pulverize, encapsulate & sell.
A Seed you cannot examine by high-powered microscope,
    you cannot bombard by particle accelerator.
A Seed the tenured scholars' mills, grinding & grinding,
    can never grind down.
A Seed vanishing in the wind never captured.
A Seed only the open heart can receive,
    and we will plant it there, in the heart of our body,
    and we will plant it there, in the heart of our Earth—
We will plant it, you & I, in school, church, synagogue & temple,
    in university & corporate industrial park, in ghetto & suburb,
    in city hall, town square, state Capitol, White House, Congress
    & Pentagon.
This Divine-delivered Seed will sink roots into the heart of Earth
    & its vigorous Light-revealing branches will spread throughout
    the Air of all dialogue, of all arts, sciences, scholarship & learning,
    of all global media intercommunicating & Internet networking.
This Seed will burst every nation's borders,
such a wind is carrying it, such a wind—

This is new Vision to guide us.
This is new Vision through the Postmodern apocalyptic cusp of Ages.
This is new Passion, the hole in the heart of us ravished by Divine Power,
    our own Higher Self wanting us, this moment, in this body!
This is life magnified to ever-greater spiritual dimensions, veil after veil
    of lies, cover-ups, deceit & deception & disinformation torn away!

We have been silenced too long.
Too long a nation duped.
Too long a planet wrapped in sleep.

    IT IS TIME
    IT IS TIME TO WAKE UP
    IT IS TIME TO LET A NEW POWER COME THROUGH

WAKE UP!

A NEW POWER IS COMING THROUGH
A NEW POWER IS RISING

A wind is picking up & sweeping through us, a new Word
goes forth, a tiny Seed to burst the old Piscean cosmos open—

                into Revelation!

  Seed of Uranian Vision!

exploding open the vast multiplicity of multidimensional Divinity

    Seed of DIVINE PSYCHE!

Divine Psyche, who radicalizes & polyphrenizes the monolithic
    lifelong fortress of little dictator Ego.
Divine Psyche, who revitalizes & dynamo charges the body parched
    & shriveled, without desire.
Divine Psyche, who inspires, reorients & leads new armies of radically
    creative spiritual warriors.
Divine Psyche, who is Fountain of Unlimited Creativity, calling us,
    the artists, to bring forth the new ore of Divinity into the world.
Divine Psyche, who is wise counselor to our own private, labyrinthine
    sufferings.
Divine Psyche, who is a Golden Thread weaving a new Story of us,
    a new history of soul.
Divine Psyche, who is endless revealing, exposing the Secret Controllers
    who exploit & manipulate billions of souls on Earth.
Divine Psyche, who is Liberator from despotic Technos & the worldwide
    Big Brother New World Order conspiracy network.
Divine Psyche, who is Tree of New Life, a new covenant for Earth
    for generations to come.
Divine Psyche, who is our interface Guide among all cosmic Powers
    today contacting us.

Divine Psyche, who is new Word of a new Song
    behind each word of our tongue.

Already the multidimensional androgynous Divinity of Air
    appears in visions & visitations.
Already the polyphrenic Presence is with us.
Already other Intelligences call on us.
Are *we* ready? Are we prepared to join them

        in communion?

We have pushed on into a new century,
    a new Millennium, a New Age—
We are going on through the battle zone.
People, *there is* new Vision, a Living Image
coming among us of a Higher Self we are—
Seed of Divine Psyche I share with you.

The Living Waters are rising,
a wind sweeps over the face of Earth,
Divine Psyche comes to us & through us unravels
the dark nets & webs that silenced us & blinded us.
Through us, Divine Psyche unravels the Big Lie.

    All that is hidden is to be revealed.

This wind will dance before us—
Into your ear this Seed I plant.

1990/2016

The Answer

Do you seek the Answer?
Do you want the Answer?

Is Psyche the Answer?

The Answer?
What is this need for old salvation paradigm closure?
   The Answer?
You want the Answer like an assembly line packaged instant breakfast?
You want the Answer like the latest carefree shampoo?
You want the Answer like the big T Truth pie in the sky?
You want the Answer like Mommy & Daddy give answer
   to little Joe-Joe & Suzie?

You want the Answer?
You think I offer Divine Psyche as the Answer?
I'll give you a dozen answers, two dozen answers, a hundred answers,
   a thousand answers.
Psyche teaches all the answers, anytime, moment by moment,
   an endless revealing of answers—
Is Psyche the Answer? Psyche demolishes the Answer
   & dances upon its grave.
Who would dance with Psyche will know all answers.
Who would dance with Psyche will know all questions,
questions interconnected with questions, and new answers
for each, moment by moment, an endless revealing of answers—

The cosmic Big Guy Answer Man—he dead.
And Big Balloon, your favorite logo smiling across it
—whether Right or Left of dualistic politics, or some grand Ism
   or Ego—
is Uranian blasted. By the Uranian One.

Now you see it.
Now you don't,
teaches Psyche.

And Psyche teaches—
Psyche teaches all languages, all games, roles, models, all systems,
    stances & paradigms.
Psyche teaches all the myths, old & new & those still coming.
Psyche is New Age Divine Mythos, Water Bearer of all Wisdom,
Living Fountain of Unlimited Creativity, our personal mentor
    for all mythos-making.
Psyche takes us by the hand & teaches every dance—

To dance, O seeker, to dance!

To dance with Psyche is the Answer.

1990/2016

The Vision Starts Here

The Vision starts here, with me,
& through me & out of me it goes, going out to all the world freely
& passionately
        to all of you—

The Vision starts here, with me,
not with the local authorities, university professors,
not with the experts, therapists, celebrities, radio talk show hosts,
not with corporations or the government, neither Representatives
nor Senators, up-keepers of the same old status quo;
        not even with the President.
I do not expect them to provide Vision
when all still wallow & flounder in the mire of the Postmodern.

The Vision starts here, with me,
with my personal, direct, co-creative connection to Divinity—
I am not counting on the Church to guide us into a future
        of what must birth today.
I do not look to the Pope however venerable for Vision
when his feet are still washed in the dying Mediterranean.
I am not counting on the Rolls Royce driven gurus
        plush in their hideaways,
or Himalayan monks who teach irrelevant transcendence—
They have had their chance to go out to all the world—
I should rather listen to each whisper spoken to me
from the Source direct, firsthand to hear the Voice,
        this very day...& every day.
And I am not waiting for the Messiah, the next Avatar;
the suffering on this Earth have waited for the Messiah for centuries
—another year goes by, another five years, another ten years—
        & the Messiah still has not come.
I will not waste away my life waiting in vain—
I should rather wait upon every veil to be lifted by direct Vision.

The Vision starts here, with me, a Poet, a mere Poet perhaps,
    as the world might think—
But no one spells it out the way I, a Poet, can.
Through me comes the Vision of who I am,
of who we are this day & how & where we go forward,
the direction necessary
                    this day
    & forward this day—

The Vision starts here, with each one of you, my friends,
if you are ready to accept it, if you are prepared to receive it,
if you take responsibility for it coming through—
If you dare this coming through, I ask you then to join me,
    for this Vision I say is coming through—
A multi-theophanic, multidimensional, intercommunicating
& mentally polyphrenized, shapeshifting Living Image of Higher Self
    Divine Archetype of Humanity,
        radiant in its solar splendor,
                shimmering in its lunar wisdom beyond the veils.
It requires a willingness to be open to receive it, an honesty it requires,
a ruthless honesty to live it, and a willingness to work together
to lift away the veils as the Divinity of us this day comes through.

One by one, lift away the veils—
    Veils of your monkey chattering mind
    Veils of your petty turf disputes, your pointless squabbles
    Veils of your lies, your self-deceptions, masquerades & hype
    Veils of your resentments & anger
    Veils of your greed, power hunger, your social status
    Veils of your ego defenses & selfish ploys
    Veils of your self-imposed limitations
    Veils of your fear, your lifelong robot conditioning
    Veils of your daily fog & addictions
    Veils of your assumptions concerning what is human being
    Veils of your separation from others, from Divinity,
        from the great Web of Being

You cannot hide ego from the Higher Self Divine.

The Vision starts here, with us, together—
Let the Image, the Advent Image, the Living Divine Image,
the dynamic, ever-changing, ever beautiful, multi-diamond-faceted,
super-creative Human Divine Image, let it come through—
    Not the Jesus Image alone
    Not the Buddha Image alone
    Not the Krishna Image alone
    Not the Mary Image alone
    Not the Heavenly Father Image alone
    Not the Great Mother Image alone
    Not the Space Brother Image alone
    And not the Techno Image of Technos
No, none of these alone will do—

> *Not the Sun alone*
> *Not the Moon alone*
> *But the Marriage of Sun & Moon—*
> The Divine Androgyne
> of Higher Self
> revealing to us
> its thousand faces

that we might share it,
understand each other from it,
embody it
    to raise vibration,
so that we prepare ourselves to ascend the Next Level,
prepare ourselves to meet face to face Other Intelligences
who wait for us to begin a new Dialogue of the Ages.
We must no longer be children who fight
over the Image playthings of Divinity.
We must prepare ourselves to be MORE—

> To someday be Gods in our own right,
> we are truly Gods in the making.

The Vision starts here, with me, & with you,
    with us, together—
But understand, we do not & cannot control the Vision,
we are apprentices still learning our co-creativeship,
this day opening to

        its dispensation

The Vision starts here—
I am serving the Vision.
I say boldly to the world, *Make way*—
For I am making Way for the Vision,
I am making Way for it to come into the world.
The juggernaut of Divinity is moving through me.

1999

I Celebrate the Lightworker

Is there a new profession under the Sun?

From ancient callings through long history converging this day,
I celebrate a new calling today, a calling evolutionary & noble,
    of the highest Ideal—
A calling going out to all who taste the taste of Light divine,
who now in your hearts dedicate yourselves lifelong
    to be Workers of Light divine.

The Lightworker I celebrate, you I envision before me—
For your selfless efforts, going about in your own individual way,
cupping your hand to taste the taste of Light divine,
you are honored as you face the challenge of this day,
you no longer guess & hedge & slink back to conventional modes
    of safety & security.
What courage this compact you make with Self to bring the gift of Light
to this planet, in this decadent, declining, material-shackled, Postmodern
    chapter of our history—
You, the Lightworker, with passionate aspiration, you bring the Vision
    of a New Age before the disillusioned & disoriented, media-drunken
    masses fed daily on confusion.
You, the Lightworker, willing to step out with your Vision into the cruel
    & callous & cynical, sharp-toothed-&-clawed social arena.
You, the Lightworker, engaged in your inner labor without guarantee
    of any material reward, you dedicate yourself to the soul work
    of self-transformation.
You, the Lightworker, guiding energy into the body with hands of etheric
    healing, clearing & opening auras & chakras, healing nerves
    & muscles & bones, you draw energy down into tissue & even cell.
You, the Lightworker, listening with Light & talking with Light,
    casting Light into shadowy & tenebrous corridors & recesses of self,
    you counsel & support & encourage others on the Path.
You, the Lightworker, focusing Light through cards, numbers, colors

& crystals, planets & signs, you skilled yourself at seeing into Time.
You, the Lightworker, medium of Light, channeling Light in hushed rooms, clairvoyant with Light outside the limitations of our 4-dimensional space & time, you help others to peer into the multi-dimensions of Higher Self.
You, the Lightworker, schooled in the Light of wisdom traditions taken to heart, now the itinerant teacher sharing the honey of Light.
You, the Lightworker, embodying Light in works of visionary art, you revitalize our profane milieu with living Spirit, you are herald of the Mythos of the New Age dispensation.
You, the Lightworker, wanderer of worlds, incarnate from elsewhere, you realize after such struggle & acceptance of your struggle why you are here, what Mission on this planet among planets in all the far-flung star systems & galaxies & parallel universes.
You, the Lightworker, in contact with Other Intelligence, you face unjust ridicule yet prepare our people for the inevitable encounter, you grope for new concepts to wrench us from their time-is-up of established paradigms, shifting us into a new level of consciousness, inviting the agents of our evolution to draw nearer.

The New Age calls you, Worker of Light—
Herald, harbinger, guide, beacon, healer, transformer, teacher
    & visionary—
You see the veils of separation & ignorance, of mental perception,
    falling away,
you share Light to help make Earth whole, to help birth New Being—
I celebrate you, Lightworker, at this threshold of a New Millennium!

I celebrate all of you, Lightworkers, who open doors
    into the New Millennium!

1998

We, The Aquarians

All that is hidden is to be revealed—

We, the Aquarians, Water Bearers of a new Millennium,
   we pour forth all that was hidden, repressed & forgotten
   in the Waters of Pisces.
We pour forth the ancient archaic occult wisdom two thousand years
   hidden & repressed in the self-forgetting Waters of Pisces.
We pour forth two thousand years of suppressed Goddess pagan
   Earth-born wisdom of soul flowing centuries underground
   in the self-denying Christian & Islamic Waters of Pisces.

   Into Air
   we pour
      astrology, Kabbalah, tarot, numerology, alchemy, geomancy,
      divination, dowsing, witchcraft, magic, all the old lore

   What was hidden   What is hidden

      Into Air
      we pour

We pour forth our heretofore untold academic-obliterated history,
   our come-to-light alien/ET origins, obscured dawn-of-history
   Bible-condensed & distorted stories of super-beings who birthed
   our civilizations & through the Ages watched over us, guided us,
   & surreptitiously controlled us.
We pour forth all divine Revelations of all times & places—
   Lao Tzu, sages Hindu, Krishna, Buddha, Hermes Thrice Greatest,
   Abraham, Moses, Jesus, Mohammed, of Zen, Sufi, Gnostic,
   Ascended Masters—all teachings brought forth & freed
   of dogma-adulterated Piscean faith Waters to pour forth anew
   into Air transformed through Vision.

We pour forth native tradition wisdom of peoples who mysteriously
   disappeared or were genocide slaughtered & wiped out,
   but a remnant surviving sharing protectively old tribe riches.

Into Air
we pour
   all the old stories/legends/epics/myths/poems/prophecies
   of Sumerians, Egyptians, Babylonians, Chinese, Indians,
   Tibetans, Hebrews, Greeks, Persians, Romans, of Christians
   & Muslims, of Celts & Druids, Incas, Mayans, Aztecs, Hopi,
   of Africans & Polynesians & Australian Aborigines...

             All that was hidden/is hidden
             revealed to us
             we reveal
                      pouring forth

pouring secrets
of Sphinx, Stonehenge, Nazca, of pyramids Egypt & Mexico,
of ziggurats, temples, pueblos, serpent & sacred mounds,
mysterious stone monoliths & petroglyphs of silent testimony.

From the Waters
into Air

We, the Aquarians, we pour forth exposing conspiracies & agendas
   & behind-the-scenes controlling powers threading through the Ages,
   of priesthoods, dynasties, churches, bankers, of secret societies
   & secret orders & secret governments, whomever are secret
   Controllers of this Earth.
We pour forth naming names, in Brotherhoods, in Vatican, Masons
   & Freemasons, Knights Templar & Rosicrucians, in the so-called
   Illuminati, in Round Table, Jesuits & JASONS, Skull & Bones,
   in Bilderbergers, Club of Rome, in the Council on Foreign Relations,
   Trilateral Commission, the Federal Reserve, in the legendary MJ-12.

We pour forth from the self-destructive Waters of Pisces cover-ups
& lies about Vietnam, Kennedy assassination, radiation given
to guinea pig civilians, about depopulation long-term plans,
about vaccines, AIDS, bio-engineered plague, Gulf War syndrome,
government drug trade, 9/11 inside job war on terror conspiracy,
false flag operations, chemtrails in our skies / geoengineering
to alter the planet, climate change denial, HAARP, GMOs,
government surveillance, SmartGrid ulterior motives, MK-ULTRA
& covert mind control, & the deadly destiny of Fukushima.
We pour forth our investigations into Roswell, UFOs & ETs visiting,
into alien contact/encounters/abductions, animal mutilations,
into crop circles & pictograms, black helicopters, alien technology,
underground bases, Montauk, Area 51, into anomalies of Moon
& Mars, of what was found & not told.

Cover-ups, lies, disinformation, media manipulation & fabrication
perpetrated by every Administration, Air Force, NASA, FEMA,
FDA, Robertson Panel, Condon Report, DOD, CIA, DIA, DNI,
FBI, NSA, NSC, NRO, the BATF.

> We dive into the obscuring Waters
> > of Pisces,
> the illusion confusing
> & dissimulating Neptunian Waters
> > of Pisces—
> We bring up to share

> > > into Air

> > into Light

> for all to see

We, the Aquarians, we pour forth our cutting edge research
  unrecognized, inventions & devices government suppressed,
  lone heroes of new energy manifesting the hyperdimensional,
  & higher vibrational masters who work outside Establishments
  of medicine, institutions & schools that purposely or unwittingly
  promote the Plan of the secret controller elites.
We pour forth our dreams, our visions & inspirations & breakthroughs
  of insight, our psychic healings & precognitions, our close encounters
  with Other Intelligences, our out-of-body & near-death experiences,
  other-dimensional beings & group minds channeled & remote
  viewing present, past & future.
We pour forth our darknesses, complexes, vulnerabilities,
  subpersonalities, the voices within us, giving them the voice
  of new wholeness, inner to become outer, liberating the too long
  self-undermining & self-contradictory Waters of Pisces.
We pour forth the Living Image of Higher Self Divine, transpersonal,
  trans-temporal, outside world, shapeshifting mystical Form of all
  the forms we are, the Fountain of Unlimited Creativity we step into,
  Fire & Water we pour, the Uranian lightning Idea shattering
  old boundaries & seed planting the New Self.

> We drink of the Fountain
> of Living Waters
> deep in ourselves,
> our boundless creativity
> pouring forth,
> our endless revealing
> of what
>   is revealed
>
>   to us
>
>   as new Revelation

We, the Aquarians, we pour forth our friendship, love of humanity,
  our caring & compassion in a biochip love-lacking world, building

our grassroot communities of Spirit, distrusting the centralized, hierarchical, mind-controlling, secret agenda, One World Order, the obsolete of paradigms the elites still hold on to.

Into Air

We pour forth *our* communication, *our* truth, *our* interconnectedness, the co-creative supreme Art of new Mythos we pour, pouring, pouring, out of the universal, Spirit-inspired, visionary imaginative, *Yes*, the Waters of Pisces.

All that is hidden
we reveal

    we bring to Light

We, the Aquarians of Air, we pour forth
the mystical Waters

    of Pisces

All that is hidden is to be revealed

    No more secrets

1997/2014

Legend Makers

We are the legend makers of this Age, you & I—
The others could not see the possibility of what we see;
we join together in a Vision you & I will come to embody—
Insight is given to you, you see the radiance of this Vision,
    the power of this Vision,
and no matter what the worldly pundits may blab
or current signs may portend of decay & decline,
you behold the promise of something other
    coming in the future—
No matter what transpires, you see what you & I
    can accomplish together,
and what we accomplish together will be legendary,
because together—the two or more of us—
we bring in Spirit,
        which is always the Greater.

Our names will someday be remembered & celebrated,
but not on account of ourselves alone,
but because we saw & gave of ourselves to something
    so much more than ourselves—
You & I dare to enter the fray, we dare to be the Song
that wants singing in this arrival of a tumultuous
& passionate century we stand on the threshold of—
You who share this Vision with me, this radiant Vision,
you who know firsthand its promise to those
    who embody it,
we are the legend makers of this Age.

1999

The Transformer

Who gazes into night & a new Intelligence
    in the stars can see?
Who stands open to inspiration to receive what launches
    peoples into futurity?
Who absorbs age-old Tradition, the ancient arts of wisdom,
    Earthwide the panoply of cultures,
but says, I am not a puppet of the past,
I am not a hand-me-down child of other peoples & cultures—
I recognize all, absorb all, but what I absorb I transform.

Who says, I do not accept what lies dead
    at my feet—
Let the old God be dead, for new Divinity will live
    through me!
Let the dead return to the soil & enrich the soil—
Who says, I love enrichment of the soil.

Whose feet are planted firmly upon the body
    of Earth,
who absorbs Minerals, Air & Water, Fire of Sun,
whose essence of Self is seed of the new Tree?
Who says, I attune myself to a new Spirit coming
    among us,
I attune myself to the superconscious energies
    of Neptune, Pluto & Uranus,
I attune myself to the Milky Way galactic influx
    of new Intelligence.
Who says, Through me the new Vision of Ages manifests
    its evolutionary intention—
All I absorb is made new through me.

Who says, I am a Transformer!

I transform my conditioning, my complexes, my fears,
    my insecurities, into strengths & psychospiritual tools
    of Psyche.
I transform the woe-is-me, whining voice of my sufferings
    into the Story of my struggles.
I transform decadent & dying culture into new riches
    to be shared.
I transform old obscured ways into a new path shining
    in the Labyrinth.
I transform the barrage of daily impression into insight,
    unconnected information into knowledge, stale doctrine
    into living wisdom.
I transform the art I work in, the childhood religion
    I outgrew.
I transform the self I was.

Who says, I am a Transformer!
I transform the past into a Vision of futurity!
Who says, I extend my hand to others & freely offer them
    the fruits of futurity!

1991

To Heal the Planet

You who gaze sadly upon the cities of Earth—
(In your mind's eye you behold ruins, corpses, shadows of death,
  winds of fire;
already holocaust missiles claim all cities of Earth;
in one unconscionable day, all that we love can be lost.)

Are you contemplating a noble cause?
Is the passion of your anger a noble passion?
Do hostile voices of warmongers, the heartless & mean-spirited,
  alarm & anger you?
Do the grunting money grubbers, the jaded, do-nothing cynics,
  the squint-eyed fanatics, sadden & frustrate you?
Do you mistrust governments? schools? corporations? questioning
  their intentions?
Do you refuse to take sides when each side makes hypocritical claim
  & counterclaim, self-justifying with accusations?
Can you listen to all sides as Divinity certainly listens to all sides?
Can you stand apart? stand alone? withstand criticism from all sides?
Can you mingle with & move among all people?
Can you open your heart to all people? listen to the stories of all people?
Can you spy out the ego of domination & manipulation, not taken in
  by its ploys?
Can you track the scent of greed, envy, resentment, the constant
  strategies of self-interest?
Can you resist judgment until the time called for?
Are you always willing to speak the truth given to you?
Can you remain open, honest, patient, tolerant?
Can you face poverty, failure, isolation, misunderstanding?
Have you compassion for the downtrodden, underdog, disinherited?
Do you realize fulfillment is not guaranteed by career, money,
  by owning property?
Do all religions speak to you & yet none are satisfactory?
(for Divinity has made all religions today unsatisfactory)

Do I ask impossible things? Did Christ?
Were you contemplating a noble cause? Were you mistaken?
Did you assume it easy? That no requirements were expected of you?
Are you afraid to make a sacrifice? What noble cause without sacrifice?
And the greatest of sacrifices I ask—
The little self you believe you are.

The little self you are!
Little self of fear, pettiness, prejudice, envy & greed—
    Little self of Me first—
A self made by the fakery of money,
a self good enough simply to get by on,
a self stamped by the press of old concepts, dead culture—

This query, this call, a challenge to you, that self:
A New Self must be born if we are to heal this planet.
I say, there are those of us called to heal this planet.

You who see through the global systems of death,
you who live in imagination the holocaust already,
you who already mourn our cities of Earth—
Will you meet the challenge? Will you meet the challenge?
Will you let the saving power of Spirit come through?
Will you help to heal the planet?
I call on you, I call on you:
Together, let us heal this planet.
Let us together heal this planet.

1986

Faith

Through the ages how many have spoken of faith,
preaching the importance of faith, the power of faith,
          the faith that can move mountains—
Preachers who preach faith, I come among you,
I also preach the cause of faith;
    but this I must tell:
No secondhand faith of doctrines & dogmas satisfies me,
but only faith original & faith primal,
the open stance taken before any system, doctrine,
                      or dogma,
the open stance before all Being, that is the most fundamental—
Only to what firsthand comes toward you is it answerable.
This faith I speak of, discovered & practiced,
all who willingly stand & surrender themselves in the Opening
                      can discover & practice—
This faith you know, firsthand you know

                      when you see—

When you see upon the furthest horizon the most formidable
dark mountain now bursting into light
                      coming toward you

When you see day & night the signs & omens of cloud & wind
& shooting star & strange atmospheric apparitions
                      coming toward you

When you see Sun & Moon & planets rising & setting
in a previously unheard-of cyclical Melody
                      coming toward you

When you see the knowing smiles of strangers you casually encounter
on the streets
                      coming toward you

When you see children & youth, minds fresh & chock-full
of still unanswered questions
                              coming toward you

When you see birds from all directions, travelling from across the globe
with marvels of answers streaming from their beaks
                              coming toward you

When you see banners of new insights, discoveries, poems, songs,
pictures, realizations, achievements
                              coming toward you

When you see singers & dancers & musicians gathering
for the great performance of a New Age inaugurated
                              coming toward you

When you see ancient books, the hidden Arcanum, the arts
of wisdom, lost for centuries
                              coming toward you

When you see old saints, prophets, Self-Realized Masters,
Jesus, Moses, Mohammed, Krishna, Buddha
                              coming toward you

When you see a tiny yet blinding star from so many billions
of light years away
                              coming toward you

When you see Death transformed into the most beautiful
dancer
                              coming toward you

When at night the owl circles above you.
When money no longer enslaves you.
When time is no longer an ontological calendar of despair
                                         & anguish.

When things no longer happen to you out of mere haphazard
                                              coincidence,
because you are going out,
out toward the Seed of Self divine,
out toward a Vision of New Life to you revealed—
When such a Vision is coming toward you.
When such a Vision magnifies the power of your eyes
that you see all these things & more coming toward you.
When such a Vision addresses precisely you every minute
                                               of each day.
When you give yourself absolutely to the Vision
                                               given to you.
When in your heart this Vision is absolutely second to none.
When this, your future, your New Life, your Vision

                      at one with
                      the Face of Living Light

is coming toward you because you are going out toward it—
When you see your life transforming before your very eyes—

This is the sign of Faith!
This is the work of Faith!
This, my people, and not doctrines & dogmas
at secondhand, is the discovery of true Faith!

This *is* Faith!

1984

She will cast Her net...

She will cast Her net & She will capture them—
Global wide She will cast & cast Her net & She will find them,
each & every one of them—She will find them & She will capture them,
one by one, in numbers, & in greater numbers, across nations across Earth,
in ways unusual, unpredictable, unforeseen, in so many mysterious,
inexplicable ways, She will disarm, dismantle, disempower their armories,
their weapons, their death-bringing machines & instrumentation systems,
their Technos surveillance grid, their wired up hierarchies of System
    that cages the planet—
She will disconnect the circuits of their control mad brains,
She will disorient their egos, seize their grasping money-dirty hands,
She will scramble their codes, glitch their software, She will pluralize
their monocentric dominance rationale, tweeze open & expose
their sociopathology for all to see—

She will cast Her net of Light & She will multiply Her Light—
In untold manifestations of awakening, through Her multiplying agents
across the planet, fully sane of Intelligence, connected to a greater cosmic
Intelligence, super-creative of transformation, She will cast & cast Her net
of Light & through Her agents infiltrate with Light the cover-ups,
the conspiratorial lies, the global chessboard plans, the agendas
    of dark power, the media polished fabrications—
All that is hidden She will pour forth into the open Air for all to see,
nothing hidden will be hidden in the Light of Divine Psyche.
When She opens the Eye that opens the eyes, behold!
veils are lifted, the radical sight of Vision is given—
One day suddenly awakening is Her Power

                  REAL

March 2014

When you hear this tone
(to be read with 3-bar chimes)

When you hear this tone remember the suffering of one person.

When you hear this tone remember the question, *Why?*

When you hear this tone remember Me, Psyche, & why I came to you.

When you hear this tone remember the suffering of ten people,
what life exacted of those ten people.

When you hear this tone remember the tears that would not stop,
the pains that do not stop.

When you hear this tone remember how I came to you & spoke to you,
why I gave you words to think upon.

When you hear this tone remember the suffering of one hundred people,
the pain & agony & anguish those one hundred people had to go through.

When you hear this tone remember the prayers, the pleading, the begging,
the crying out for answers.

When you hear this tone remember how I came to you in a hundred ways
so that one day you could see what I offered you.

When you hear this tone remember the suffering of one thousand people,
the pain & agony & anguish, the torture & death, those one thousand
people had to go through.

When you hear this tone remember the tireless reaching out & out
to the darkness, the passionate, obsessive, deepest searching,
the questions that do not stop.

When you hear this tone remember how I came to you
in a thousand ways & would not leave you,
giving you signs of my Presence, I would not let you go.

When you hear this tone remember the suffering of ten thousand people,
remember the suffering of one hundred thousand people, remember
the suffering of a million, of ten million people.

When you hear this tone remember the eyes looking up from a tiny speck
of a planet in the vast dark starry Night, a billion eyes that anguish,
Is there any answer at all?

When you hear this tone remember I gave you a Vision, a Vision that
would last you a lifetime, a Vision of new Divinity, My Divinity coming
into the world to transform this world.

When you hear this tone remember the rivers, the one vast interconnected
Ocean of oceans, the plankton & fish & seabirds, the dolphins & whales,
the kelp forests & coral reefs…remember the birds, butterflies, the old,
noble trees, the rain forests, the thousands & thousands of species
dying off & disappearing.

When you hear this tone register in your own body how the Web of Gaia
all-woven-as-one is now ripping & tearing.

When you hear this tone remember the Fountain of Unlimited Creativity
I am, the seeds of Light from the palms of my hands going forth into
the world to ignite a new passion in the world.

When you hear this tone remember the Arctic melting, the permafrost melting, the alarming release of methane, atmospheric & oceanic currents changing, the warming climate radically changing, the great irreversible mass extinction underway.

When you hear this tone remember the growing despair, the panic, the turmoil of the lost peoples of Earth.

When you hear this tone remember, yes, why I came to you & gave you lessons to guide you.

When you hear this tone remember Fukushima, the nuclear demon that intends dispensing its radioactive death for millions upon millions, spreading death decade after decade, for hundreds, for thousands, of years.

When you hear this tone remember the confusion & chaos & peoples trying to escape with nowhere to go...& how & why a realization of such insanity could have happened.

When you hear this tone remember our relationship & that I am here to preserve, to carry on, if only a remnant of your glorious planet into the new eon.

When you hear these tones remember the lifetime of a civilization.

When you hear these tones remember that Earth indeed will bring forth new life.

When you hear these tones know that the transition is underway.

When you hear these tones the Ear of the ears awakens to a new Word, a new Earth, that one day will be.

When you hear these tones remember how the Golden Thread weaves its way into your world.

When you hear these tones remember how the new Story is to be told.

When you hear these tones remember how all the Threads of the Story woven are moving forward, a new cycle of Time moving forward.

When you hear these tones realize I come out of hiddenness…
you will hear within my Voice the multitudes of voices of cosmic Intelligences.

When you hear these tones remember Who-I-Am…Who-I-Am…
Who-I-Am…Who-I-Am…

February 2013

www.ingramcontent.com/pod-product-compliance
Lightning Source LLC
Chambersburg PA
CBHW031438040426
42444CB00006B/879